The
Young
Eagle

by Tom Reilly

Motivation Press
St. Louis, Missouri

Library of Congress Cataloging-in-Publication Data

Reilly, Thomas P.
    The Young Eagle/Tom Reilly
    ISBN: 0-944448-28-3

Other Books by Tom Reilly:
    Simple Psychology:
        Simple Living in a Complicated World
    Value Added Selling
    Coaching for Sales Success
    Customer Service Is More Than a Department
    Crush Price Objections

Printed in the USA by Motivation Press.

Dedication

To Charlotte, my wife. You have always been
the wind beneath my wings.

Acknowledgements

I would like to thank the following people for their help on this project: Charlotte, my wife and editor, whose eagle eye I respect; Joann and Linda, my staff associates, whose input I value; and Cathy Davis, cover design artist, whose talent captured the spirit of the Young Eagle.

PROLOGUE

The nest of Young Eagles hung on every word as the Master Eagle described his exploits. This was an important day for the eaglets. They were preparing for their first solo flight from the nest. It was the confidence builder many of them needed to fulfill their destiny.

"How far can I travel?" asked one of the eaglets.

"How far can you see?" responded the Master Eagle.

"How high can I fly?" quizzed the Young Eagle.

"How far can you stretch your wings?" asked the old eagle.

"How long can I fly?" the eaglet persisted.

"How far is the horizon?" the mentor rebounded.

"How much should I dream?" asked the eaglet.

1

"How much can you dream?" smiled the older, wiser eagle.

"How much can I achieve?" the young one continued.

"How much can you believe?" the old eagle challenged.

Frustrated by the banter, the Young Eagle demanded, "Why don't you answer my questions?"

"I did."

"Yes. But you answered them with questions."

"I answered them the best I could."

"But you're the Master Eagle. You're supposed to know everything. If you can't answer these questions, who can?"

"You," the old, wise eagle reassured.

"Me? How?" the Young Eagle was confused.

"No one can tell you how high to fly or how much to dream. It's different for each eagle. Only you and God know how far you'll go. No one on this earth knows your potential or what's in your heart. You alone will answer that. The only thing that limits you is the edge of your imagination."

The Young Eagle, puzzled by this, asked, "What should I do?"

"Look to the horizon, spread your wings, and fly."

The Young Eagle was perched on the limb that supported his home from birth. He faced the eastern sky, as he did every morning just as the sun awakened. The nascent sun lit the golden plumage of his neck and head while its warmth and glow stirred a restless and curious spirit in him. He could feel the full weight of destiny tugging at him. The Old World is a good place for a young eagle—any eagle, for that matter.

Today, he will fly alone from the nest, beginning his solo journey. *Fear is just another word for excitement*, he thought. The Young Eagle felt both. He turned his head to steal one last look at the sleeping nest dwellers. They were not ready for their solo flights from the nest—their time will come. Today is all about the Young Eagle's journey. The Young Eagle has been preparing for this day since he broke free from the shell. He built his wing strength by jumping from one limb to another. He flew with the Master Eagle to learn how to soar, hunt, and read the thermals. He studied the habits of other predators as well as prey. He has mentally rehearsed this journey dozens of times. The anticipation for this day has been overwhelming for a fledgling. Destiny demands a great deal from the young, and youthful zeal leaves little room for patience. Starting a new life, beginning a new journey, leaving the familiar and comfortable are scary and exciting. Soon, the Young Eagle will learn that he needs the energy from both of these emotions—fear and excitement—to sustain him on his journey.

He replayed his many lessons with the Master Eagle: "Many eagles fail to leave the security of their nests because of fear. They fear the unknown. They don't realize that fear is part of the excitement. By avoiding their fears, they also avoid life's pleasant surprises. In the great unknown, opportunity lives and waits for them. How can they seize these opportunities if they live out of fear?"

"What else are they afraid of?" the Young Eagle pressed.

"For many, it's the idea of change. They're comfortable where they are—in their nests. They don't want to push themselves. Maybe no one encouraged them to dream or stretch their wings as far as they could. For others, change means leaving something or someone behind—friends, family or the security of the nest. Starting anew means leaving the old."

"I've not thought much about what I will leave behind. Now that I'm thinking about it, it makes me kind of sad to think of leaving everyone."

"You will take your memories and their spirit with you, and there's a very good chance you will return one day. Many young eagles do."

"Will I be scared when I leave?"

"Probably, and that's okay. Fear can be your friend or your foe. If you let it overpower you, it becomes your foe. If it sharpens your senses and makes you vigilant, it is your friend. It will protect you as long as you don't let it overpower you. Feel the fear and use its energy to help you fly. There will be times on the journey that you will need the boost."

The Young Eagle smiled at these memories. He was fond of the teacher who nudged him. The Master Eagle believed in this young bird, and that made the Young Eagle believe in himself. That was the greatest gift the Master Eagle could give the Young Eagle—self-confidence. This confidence empowered the Young Eagle and gave him the courage to leave the nest. He would need both confidence and courage for the journey that lies ahead.

The Master Eagle's words from their last conversation hung on the walls of the Young Eagle's memory: "Look to the horizon, spread your wings, and fly."

I can't stay in this nest forever, the Young Eagle thought. *Every eagle must fly. It's my time. It's impossible to reach great heights without venturing from the nest. The longer I stay in this nest, the harder it will be for me to leave.*

With that, the Young Eagle stretched his wings as wide as they would go, fully exposing a brilliant white underside that matched his tail. His reach seemed broader today, foretelling his ascent to great heights. He caught air and felt the thermals lift him effortlessly. One thousand meters. Two thousand meters. Three thousand meters. Beyond. This is the highest the Young Eagle has ever flown. He felt the release of the fear that once pulled at him like gravity. The Master Eagle's words made more sense now. Fear can keep eagles close to the ground and close to the nest. As he released his fear, he was able to soar to unfamiliar heights. Fear no longer held him back. The Young Eagle was learning a valuable lesson: As he concentrated on flying, he left fear in his wake. He was flying away from it. This intense focus left little room for fear.

His wings cut deep into the air with little resistance. The air felt cool and crisp. He filled his lungs fully with the pure, high air. The high air smelled fresher and it tasted different. His vision clearly pierced this high air all the way to the edge of the horizon. *It's quieter up here*, he thought. The Young Eagle discovered another of nature's great lessons: The higher an eagle soars, the less crowded the sky. He owned the sky. This was his domain and he was master. It was all new and exciting, just as the Master Eagle had promised. *Fear is just another word for excitement*, he reminded himself. *I never would have experienced this had I submitted to my fear.*

"Hey, Youngster," the gravelly voice startled the Young Eagle.

"What? Who are you? Where did you come from?" the Young Eagle asked, visibly shaken.

Who is this intruder? he thought.

"Oh, I've been around for a while. I was watching you earlier."

"What do you mean you were watching me?"

The Young Eagle thought: *What gives this eagle the right to watch me do anything?*

"I was circling while you were still in the nest this morning."

"Why would you circle over our nest?"

"Oh, a friend of yours asked me to keep an eye out for you."

"Who?"

"Your Master Eagle, of course."

"How do you know him?"

"He and I used to fly together. In our younger days, we traveled great distances together. In fact, we made the great journey east together, just like you're doing. Now, I hover about and keep an eye on the young ones like yourself when you first leave the nest."

This reference to the Master Eagle relaxed the Young Eagle. He was relieved to hear that the intruder knew the Master Eagle.

"I thought I was on my own," the Young Eagle said defiantly.

"You are. But that doesn't mean you are alone. There are others along your journey to help you as you need it."

"Is that your job?"

"Yes, one of them."

"So, there are others like you out there?"

"Oh, yes. And you will meet several in your travels. Like the Master Eagle, they will help you learn the lessons every Young Eagle must learn."

"What lessons? I thought I already got that from the Master Eagle."

The older eagle smiled. *Youth!* he thought.

"Learning doesn't stop when you leave the nest. That's when it really starts."

"Oh," the Young Eagle responded.

Like many young eagles, this one thought he knew everything he needed to know, but soon would learn that leaving the nest began the next phase of his education.

"There are six things you must learn on your journey. At various stops along your journey, you will encounter a mentor and learn one of the six things that every eagle must know. Once you have learned all six of them, your future will be as clear as this high air. For now, you're just flying around, right?"

"Yeah, I thought that's all there was to it. You know, spread my wings and fly."

"You will discover there's more to your journey than catching air and bumping into clouds."

"What else is there?"

"The great truth awaits you. You will discover it along with your destiny."

"What is the great truth?" the Young Eagle demanded.

"In time, my young friend. When you are ready, you will learn it."

"What should I do now?"

"Look to the horizon, spread your wings, and fly."

With that, the older eagle packed his wings snugly against his body and dove vertically, falling thousands of meters. The Young Eagle marveled at his swift and graceful descent.

Look to the horizon, spread your wings, and fly. I've heard that before. The winds aloft interrupted his thought: *I can ride these winds forever. That's what the Master Eagle told me, always seek the winds—fly them, let their momentum carry you, use them.*

The Young Eagle danced his aerial ballet—falling, turning, tumbling, climbing, and rolling. The older eagle watched from a distance, admiring the youthful play.

After playing with the thermals, the Young Eagle turned to the eastern sky, caught air and streaked across a clear, blue sky. The Young Eagle reflected on his early lesson that it is easier to soar to grand heights because so few birds try. It surprised him that it wasn't as crowded as he thought it might be: *How could others not want to experience this?*

With his vision as keen as ever, the Young Eagle saw as far as his imagination allowed, beyond the edge of the horizon. Things looked clear up here. Things just seemed to fit when viewed from a distance. There was a pattern to how everything—trees, rivers, fields, mountains—fit together. It's as if some master artist painted this grand design. Colors and patterns blended magically and seamlessly into a natural palette of sky and earth.

Experiencing nature's wonders caused the Young Eagle to think: *How did all of this come about? How did a tree know how to be a tree? How did a river know how to flow and find its way from one end to another? Why did this mountain decide to reach for the sky? Why do eagles want to fly? Why do fish swim? Maybe these are the things I will learn along the way?*

The Young Eagle spotted dark clouds in the eastern sky and felt the wind tugging hard on his left wing. He could smell the storm building. The air felt heavier before a storm and lighter after a cleansing. It was time to find somewhere to ride out the storm. The Young Eagle spotted a clump of trees on the southern side of a hill and knew that would be his refuge—a place of safety to watch the rains. He curled his wings and dove for the trees. He landed gracefully on a middle limb, shielded from the storm but still part of it.

"It's a great storm, isn't it?"

The Young Eagle was startled to see an owl sitting on a nearby branch. "Yes, it is. You know, I used to be afraid of these things," the Young Eagle said nervously.

"Yeah, me too," smiled the owl. "Is this your first trip by yourself?"

"Yeah, how did you know?"

"Oh, I know. I've seen many birds on their first trip. What do you think so far?"

"I think there's a lot I don't know. For instance, today I learned that when I'm soaring high things look different. Everything seems to fit naturally in a design or a pattern."

"They do, and it's easier to see that the farther away you get," the owl confirmed.

"How long do you think this storm will last?"

The impatience of youth always amuses birds that have been around for a while. The owl said, "Until it's finished."

"That's a strange answer."

"Not really. The storm has its place, like everything. It cleanses and nourishes. It will rain for a while and stop when it's time to stop. That's how it works."

"That's how what works?"

"The world. Life," said the owl. "It all fits together, just like you said."

The Young Eagle paused to reflect on this thought when a bolt of lightning lit the sky and a clatter of thunder broke the silence. The Young Eagle jumped.

"Everything fits together?"

"Absolutely. For example, when you woke up this morning, where did the sun rise?"

"In the eastern sky."

"Of course. Where will it sleep tonight?"

"In the western sky."

"Exactly. It does that every day, as it has since the beginning of time. What follows winter?"

"Spring, of course," the Young Eagle offered with a whiff of youthful sarcasm.

"And what follows spring?"

"Summer."

"And what follows summer?"

"Please, fall." The Young Eagle's impatience with these questions overwhelmed his manners.

"Yes, as they have since the beginning of time. That's The Plan."

"What plan?" asked the Young Eagle.

"The Plan for the universe. It's the same plan that will bring out the stars and moon tonight, as it has done since the beginning of time. Without this plan, the world and the universe would be in chaos, but they're not. Things are perfectly ordered, according to The Plan."

The Young Eagle soaked up this conversation like the dry ground soaked up the rain.

"Is that how trees know how to grow and fish know how to swim?"

"Yes, and it's how you know to fly. There is a grand plan for the universe and you are part of it, my friend, just like everything else. It's why you're here at this moment talking to me, resting on your journey. It's why the storm brought you here."

"That's a pretty big thing to think about. How can all of this be so structured? What could account for all of this?"

"That's the power, my friend."

"The power? What power?"

"The power of God. Nothing short of an all-powerful God could make all of this happen. That is the wonderful lesson in nature. It was all created by God and governed by The Plan. Everything is part of it. Your journey has been around since the beginning of time. God knew your journey when He created all of this. You play an important role in time. That's why you're here at this moment."

"I never thought much about that. I didn't know I was *that* important."

"You *are* that important. That's why you're here. You fit into things. You're a part of all of this. An important part. You have a role to play. You have a destiny. And God has known this destiny since the beginning of time. He knew you before he formed you in the shell."

This made the Young Eagle shiver and smile, but it was a lot for a Young Eagle to think about. The importance and magnitude of his life would take time to sink in.

"Did you think life was nothing more than a couple of birds bumping into each other from time to time?" asked the owl.

"I don't know. Uh, I never really thought about any of this. I mean, today I wondered how trees knew to be trees and rivers knew how to run in a certain direction and why mountains reached to the sky. Leaving the nest is a new adventure for me. Heck, when I woke up this morning I just started flying east, not thinking much about it."

"I understand how that feels. I, too, had to leave the nest as a young owl."

"So, where do I fit in?"

"That's part of your journey—to figure that out. I can't tell you."

"What's your place in all of this?" the Young Eagle asked.

"To do what I am doing right now."

"Doing what?"

"Teaching you your first lesson on your journey, just as the old eagle promised."

Mentioning the old eagle and the lesson to be learned surprised, yet reassured, the Young Eagle. He thought: *It is like all of this had been planned from the start. Isn't that what the owl was saying? There is a plan, The Plan, and all things fit together as part of it.*

"Do I have a choice in all of this?" asked the Young Eagle.

"Sure, you do. You always have a choice. That, too, is part of The Plan."

"But what if I decide to go back to the nest and stop my journey here?"

"You can do that if you wish, and many have.

The problem is then you will deprive yourself and the rest of us of the meaning and the purpose of your destiny."

"The rest of us? Who are the rest of us? What does that mean?" asked an incredulous Young Eagle.

"We have been waiting for you for some time. Your destiny is as much a part of our lives as it is yours. You bring something that nothing else in this world brings. As a world, we are better off because of you. That's how very special you are."

The Young Eagle shivered again. "It makes me tingle to think about being that special."

"You *should* tingle because you are that special. It should really make you tingle to know that you're an important part of something much bigger than a single bird on a flight. We are all connected in our destinies and purpose."

"So, where or how do I find out about my destiny?"

"Look to the horizon, spread your wings, and fly."

The Young Eagle slept well the first night on his journey. A full day of flying and a spectacular storm always helps a bird sleep. He awakened to the first light of day. He rose to his talons and stretched his wings. It felt like his wings grew wider and stronger overnight. The Young Eagle faced the eastern sky and watched the rising sun. It rose in the east, just as it had done every day since the beginning of time.

That's what the owl said last night, the Young Eagle thought. He looked around for his storm companion, but the owl was gone. That didn't surprise the Young Eagle. He figured the owl had done his job and left, maybe to help another Young Eagle on his or her first day of flight.

I liked what the owl said last night about my destiny. I feel important today. It's peaceful and secure and exciting to know that there is a scheme of things in the whole scheme of things. There is a rhyme and reason for all of this and all of us. There must be an organizing force because all of this had to come from somewhere. Something can't come from nothing. I'm hungry. It's time to fly and hunt.

In a flash, he swooped on his unsuspecting prey. As the Young Eagle was finishing his meal, he heard an unfamiliar voice.

"You're a skillful hunter. I watched you dive for your prey. Few could escape the skill and speed of your prowess," said the onlooker.

The hawk startled the Young Eagle who withdrew into a defensive posture.

"No need to fear, young hunter. I'm not here for your food. I was admiring the swiftness of your technique."

"That's flattering coming from one of the most brilliant hunters on earth," the Young Eagle echoed the compliment. "I did good?"

"You ate well, didn't you?"

"Yes."

"Then, you did fine."

The Young Eagle relaxed a bit, an observation that did not escape the hawk.

"Solo flight, eh?"

"Yes, how did you know?" asked the Young Eagle, surprised at the hawk's observation.

"Oh, I know. I've seen it before. It's all part of the scheme of things."

Another lesson, the Young Eagle thought.

"So, you're one of my teachers?"

"Yes, I am. What have you learned so far?"

"I know that there are six lessons. There is a scheme of things called The Plan, and I'm an important part of it." The Young Eagle beamed with pride.

"Right you are, young fella. Your part is your destiny. You're here for a reason."

The Young Eagle impatiently interrupted, "Is that your lesson for me? Are you going to tell me what my destiny is?"

"No," sighed the hawk. "Your Master Eagle told you that was between you and God and that no one could tell you your destiny, didn't he?"

"Yeah," the Young Eagle hung his head in disappointment.

"You must understand that if someone gave you your destiny, it wouldn't be your destiny. It would be their destiny for you. Does that make sense?"

"Yeah, sort of. I guess it makes sense. But how will I know?"

"You will know, I promise. That's what this journey is all about—discovering for yourself that special purpose for why you're here. You really are a brilliant hunter."

The conversation turned as quickly as the Young Eagle dove for food. "Yeah, it sort of comes natural to me."

"That's the way it is in The Plan."

"That's the way what is?"

"What comes natural for you is different than what comes natural for others."

"Uh huh," mumbled the Young Eagle.

"Your destiny is different than other birds; therefore, you must have different talents. You are different from every other eagle that ever flew or ever will fly. That's The Plan. You are unique, just like the rest of us. No other eagle will fly your path or see what you see. Since the first time you turned your head in a different direction from the other eaglets in your nest, you began to view the world differently. You have already experienced more on your short trip than the fledglings you left behind."

"My life is different. I know that. I've sensed it from the start."

"Of course, it is."

"I'm anxious to see where this journey will take me."

"Youthful exuberance is truly a gift. That's part of the excitement—the discovery. You will learn things about this world your imagination could not have convinced you of. You will learn things about yourself that you can learn only when you're on the journey. You have talents and skills you don't even know about yet. They will surface along the way. That's why this is so exciting. Discovery is an important part of the journey."

The Young Eagle liked what he heard. The hawk was one of the fastest-flying birds in the sky. The Young Eagle knew this from his lessons with the Master Eagle, but he was pleasantly surprised to discover how encouraging this hawk could be. It made sense that the hawk would support him. They were cousins, of course. It felt good to be around another bird who was optimistic about the Young Eagle's journey. He could draw from this support. This made the Young Eagle feel even more excited about his journey.

"What do you like to do?"

"I love to fly and explore. Yesterday, I flew higher than ever before and it was exciting. Today, I will stretch my wings beyond yesterday. I am really curious how high I can fly."

"That's the right attitude, young friend. You build confidence every time you stretch beyond your past. Your past is not your potential. I was always curious how fast I could fly," the hawk shared with the Young Eagle.

"Things look different the higher I fly. It's like they are clearer. I can see farther the higher I go. I can see the edge of the horizon."

"You are a skilled flyer and a magnificent hunter I can tell that. You remind me of another traveler I met years ago, when I was just a fledgling. He was a great soaring bird, too. Graceful. Entertaining. And fast, like you. My brothers, sisters and I would sit in our nest and watch him dance on the currents. He would catch air and dance like no other eagle I've seen. Watching him soar made all of us wonder how much speed and skill each of us had in us. He inspired us with his talent. He stuck around for a while and then continued on his journey east. We knew he was too grand an explorer for our little piece of the sky. We always wondered what happened to him."

The Young Eagle listened anxiously to this story. He could imagine himself soaring and entertaining others with his ballet of flight. He dreamed of visiting distant places. He was this type of explorer

"I could do that," he caught himself thinking aloud.

The hawk grinned at this youthful innocence and openness. "Yes, you can and should. If you can imagine it, it is real for you. You must travel. You are filled with possibilities. You have a lot of exploring in you. Listen to your heart. Go where it tells you to go. Your talent will call out to you, and to discover your destiny, you must answer that call. You are special, and because of that, you are blessed with special talents and skills. I call them destiny's tools. They will be your traveling companions on this journey. They will guide you and support you. Expressing them is why you're here. It's all part of The Plan."

"How will I know these talents?"

"You'll know. There are some things that are so effortless for you that you will amaze even yourself at times. You'll wonder why you possess such great gifts. You'll ask yourself, 'Why have I been so blessed?' Then, you'll realize why you're here. The talents you possess are your talents alone. No other bird will be able to do things exactly the way you do them. Your talents are special and unique, just as you are special and unique. These talents are God's gift to you. What you do with these talents is your gift to God."

Optimism is one of life's greatest natural stimulants and these positive words of the hawk worked magically. The Young Eagle could barely contain his impatience. "How soon will I discover this?"

"It will take as long as it takes. Exploring your world, discovering your talents and learning from these experiences are part of the process of becoming who you are meant to be. Just because you finished your lessons with the Master Eagle doesn't mean that you stop learning. There are lessons you learn in the nest and lessons you learn on your journey. Your nest lessons prepared you for your next lessons." The hawk impressed himself with his poetic choice of words.

The hawk continued, "You will discover that finding success on this journey requires humility on your part."

"I don't understand. I thought I am supposed to feel proud of being special?"

"You are. Be proud of who you are and what you accomplish. Balance that pride with a humility that encourages you to grow and learn. Creatures that lack humility never really discover all of what they can become because they think they know it all—that they are finished learning and growing."

This puzzled the Young Eagle. Like most Young Eagles, he wanted answers to all of his questions, and he wanted them now. But the answers would not come now—only more questions for the journey.

"I'm not sure where I'll go next but I am feeling a pull in some direction."

"Go with the pull. You're young. See where it takes you. That's the art of discovery. You have the heart and talent for exploration. I can tell by just talking with you."

"Yes, I do and I will. This makes sense to me. Thank you."

"Thank you, young explorer. I admire your enthusiasm. It reminds me of how I felt as a young bird—full of energy. Every time I have this conversation with Young Eagles, I feel refreshed. You see, this is my destiny, to help young birds who are on their journeys. Your enthusiasm reminds me of why I do this. Now, I only have one thing more for you."

The Young Eagle leaned forward to hear this important message, "Yes, what is it?"

"Look to the horizon, spread your wings, and fly."

The Young Eagle arched his back, stretched his wings, and caught air. He circled a few times for the hawk to witness his talent for flying, dipped one wing and reached for the horizon.

The Young Eagle rose to the eastern sun, as he had done every day since birth. The eastern sky called to him. His destiny. The Young Eagle drank in the morning air—crisp, invigorating. It was the fuel he needed for a long day of flight. He traveled longer distances each day, expanding the reach of his domain. This was truly his transcendent journey. He could feel his wings getting stronger and his vision sharper. He was learning as he flew his journey. Each day prepared him for the next. His confidence grew with each new experience. He was becoming more and more of what he was born to be.

I've learned a lot so far. I understand that there is a plan for this world. That it was created by God.

I am an important part of this plan. I am on this earth for a reason, and that reason is locked away in my destiny. This makes me feel special, knowing that no other eagle has my purpose; no other eagle will fly my journey. I can be proud of this, but I must balance my pride with humility, realizing that I am a part of something much bigger than a single eagle on his journey.

I am possessed by uniqueness. There are no other birds like me anywhere. And because I am unique, others must be unique as well, and for me to appreciate my uniqueness, I must accept the uniqueness of other birds. We are made that way for our special destinies. To criticize their uniqueness is to criticize The Plan. Because I'm special, I have talents that are mine. No other bird can do what I do exactly as I do it. My experiences so far in this short life have prepared me for this. My talents are my gifts from God. These are blessings. And I must use them. How I use them is my way of thanking God for these gifts. I've never felt so special in my life. To be a vital part of something much bigger than me gives me a sense of purpose. This purpose must be my destiny. How will I know what to do? This is the question I must answer. I will search for this answer. I will fly east for the answer.

This was a good day for flying and thinking. There is much for the Young Eagle to learn on this journey. Some days, eagles need alone time to think about where they've been and where they're headed. A bird learns so much that it can overwhelm. It takes time for all these lessons to sink in and make sense. This was that type of day for the Young Eagle.

The air was especially clear today and the thermals were strong. The Young Eagle soared to new heights, and like every other time he reached a new height, he was struck by how ordered things appeared. Things just seem to fit in nicely.

The Young Eagle settled in for the evening. It was the longest day of flying yet. He was especially tired this evening. He felt more like an eagle in training than an eagle on a journey. Then, he remembered what the hawk said about continuous learning. He ate and drank sparingly today, teaching himself discipline and preparing for long periods of flight without rest, food or water. He was testing his limits and building his confidence.

The moon was full and stars dotted the sky. They seemed to multiply every night. As he sat in the mighty oak, he found it difficult to keep his eyes open. They were as heavy as the nightfall. He relented and fell into a deep and restful sleep.

"Long day?"

"Uh, yes." The Young Eagle looked around to see where the voice came from. "Where are you?"

"You're sleeping my friend. This is a dream."

"Who are you?"

"Look at the sky. I am the voice of the stars."

"When did stars start talking?"

"When did eagles start talking?"

Fair enough, the Young Eagle thought.

"So, I'm dreaming?"

"Yes. It's time to rest. And learn."

"What am I supposed to learn in my sleep?"

"Maybe what you already know but don't yet understand. Maybe it's your destiny talking to you. Maybe you're learning your place in The Plan."

"Do you know my destiny? Can you tell me what it is?"

"No. No one can tell you your destiny. You know that."

"I know, but I thought I might as well ask. What should I do?"

"Listen."

"That's all?"

"That's everything. Listen to the silence. What calls to you from the deep silence of your soul?"

"I don't know. How can silence call to me?"

"From the deep silence comes wisdom. You will know when you hear it. Listen closely."

The Young Eagle fell deeper into his sleep. He waited in silence for the voice of night. Time had no meaning here. Deeper into his sleep. Listening for the deep silence.

"You must dream."

"Of course, I must dream. I'm doing that right now," the Young Eagle replied in his sleep.

"You must dream beyond your sleep."

"What does that mean?"

"Dreaming is not just for nighttime while sleeping. It is for daytime and for while you're living. You must dream for your life."

"I must have dreams for my life?"

"Yes, you must dream fully for your life. You must have dreams to help fulfill your destiny."

"How much should I dream?"

"Didn't your Master Eagle already answer that for you?"

"Yes. He said, 'How much *can* you dream?' It really wasn't much of an answer."

"It was the right answer. You must dream big dreams for yourself. The bigger the better. That's why you are blessed with a creative intellect—to dream big dreams. Using your creative intellect takes practice, just like when you jumped from branch to branch to build your wing strength. The more you use your imagination, the stronger it becomes."

"How big is big?"

"You have a lot of questions, don't you? You don't have to ask anyone or anything for permission to dream big. That is your right. Dream big enough to make your bones itch."

This made the Young Eagle giggle when he thought about his bones itching.

"Dream about your destiny. Dream so big that the only way you will fly there is with the help of God."

"That's pretty big. I've never thought that big before."

"Most birds don't. How far would you fly if you knew you wouldn't fail on your journey?"

"I would fly beyond the edge of the horizon and back. I would explore the far reaches of my imagination." The Young Eagle recalled the words of the Master Eagle.

"Yes, that's right. That's how big you must dream. And it must be *your* dream, not another's dream for you, just as your destiny is not the same as another's destiny."

"I know I have special talents and a place in The Plan. I've learned that on my journey."

"That's true. And one of these special talents is your ability to dream. It's a power only you possess for you. You must dream *your* dreams."

"How will I know when they are my dreams?"

"You will know because you will lose yourself in your dreams. These dreams will cause your blood to race through your veins and your heart to thunder in your chest."

"And my bones itch?" The Young Eagle giggled again.

"Yes, exactly. Your bones will itch. Treat yourself to the big dream."

"I do dream. Other eagles have told me I'm a dreamer. I thought they were making fun of me, but I didn't care. I like to dream."

"That's good. Be careful about listening to others when it comes to your dreams. They don't share your passion or talents. They cannot give you permission to dream. They may not know what's best for you. They may dream small and want you to do the same. Small dreamers always want others to dream small. It makes them feel big."

"Back in the nest, the other young eagles told me I was thinking too bold to want to fly from the nest this soon."

"That's what happens. Others may be timid where you are bold or weak where you are strong. It doesn't make your dreams wrong for you, just wrong for them. That's why they protest. Do you know what the oughta's and shoulda's are?"

"No."

"It's when other birds tell you that you oughta do this or shoulda done that. They are commenting on or criticizing your dreams and what they think you should do. Remember, their opinion does not ordain your potential. Listen for good information, but don't let their comments limit or inhibit you. How can they know what's in your heart? How can they know what's best for you?"

"That sounds familiar."

"This is one of life's most important lessons, and it's good to learn it early on your journey. Others' dreams are their dreams, not yours. Your dreams are your dreams, not theirs. Why would you give other birds the power to criticize your dreams or limit your imagination?"

"That's right. There are things I want to do and places I want to go that scared the other eaglets in our nest."

"You can't let their fears become your fears or you will never fly to your dreams. And if you don't fly to your dreams, you will never live your destiny."

"So, I guess this is my next lesson, right? To dream great big dreams that are my dreams?"

"Yes, that is your next lesson. And one more thing."

"What's that?"

"Look to the horizon, spread your wings, and fly."

The Young Eagle stirred in his sleep as these familiar words nudged him. As he stirred, a star in the eastern sky smiled brightly, welcoming the eastern sun. Destiny awaits him. Truth is on the horizon.

The Young Eagle hung around this oak for weeks, flying daily shorts but always returning to his perch, trying to relive the conversation in his dream. The message inspired him to dream big dreams. Each day his dreams grew bigger than the day before. As he opened his mind to dreaming big, the ideas flowed freely. *So many dreams, so little time*, he thought. He dreamed big things and his bones often itched, which made him smile. He felt peaceful and inspired in this place. It was familiar and comforting—a good resting place on his journey. His thoughts refreshed and inspired him.

Every day, the Young Eagle awakened to the eastern sun and fell asleep to the eastern star. He spent his days exploring new places, soaring to new heights and gathering sticks and twigs for the nest he built. He was building a life for himself, but he was lonely. He was alone and missed his friends back in the nest and the time he spent with his Master Eagle. He was on his own now. Being so totally dependent on himself was new and different than he imagined. His future hinged on the decisions he would make and the actions he would take. He was discovering one of nature's most important lessons: success in pursuing his dreams rests squarely on the back of the Young Eagle.

The nest he built was strong and safe. Even though he would not live in this nest for long, it would serve many other birds on their journeys. Building a nest and leaving it behind for others to enjoy made him feel good. It was his gift to other travelers. He felt connected to them by sharing the results of his labors.

At the end of a long day, the Young Eagle rested in the nest and dreamed of travels to distant places. The explorer in him called out to the Young

Eagle often. His dreams were attempts to answer this call.

Today, the Young Eagle noticed that a sparrow had joined him in the oak. He watched as the sparrow busily built a home. At first, they nodded to each other, cautiously checking out the other. The Young Eagle had encountered many sparrows on his journey but never spent much time with them. After a while the Young Eagle, lonely and eager for company, seized the opportunity to start a conversation.

"You're a pretty busy bird, aren't you?"

"Sure am. I've got to build this nest for the mating season."

"Oh, right," the Young Eagle demurred.

"What are you doing here?"

"On my journey."

"Yeah, where are you headed?"

"Lots of places. Just haven't figured it all out yet. But I'm working on it."

"I see. So, you're getting ready to get ready?" the sparrow chirped.

"Yeah, I guess you could say that." The Young Eagle was embarrassed by the sparrow's observation. "So, what's your story?"

"Well, like I said. I'm building my nest for the mating season. I can't mate if I don't have a nest for my babies."

"I don't have a family yet. I'm still, uh. . ."

"Searching?"

"Yes, searching. I'm an explorer. That's one of my talents. I'm really good at it. It's a gift."

"We all have 'em."

"Gifts, you mean?"

"Yep."

"What's yours?"

"I love to sing."

"No kidding? Let me hear you," the Young Eagle pleaded.

With that, the sparrow shared her song with the Young Eagle. It touched him. He had never heard anything this beautiful before.

"Wow. That's beautiful. It made my feathers twitch."

The sparrow dipped her head modestly, acknowledging the compliment. "Thank you. I love to sing. It's what I was born to do."

"You do it beautifully. I get it. Singing is your destiny?"

"It's my passion and my calling. My destiny is to share it with the rest of the world. That's why I'm here."

"You're lucky."

"Why do you say that?"

"Because you know what your destiny is and you're living it. I wish I knew my destiny."

"You will. You'll discover it."

"When? Can you help me? Do you know my destiny?"

"No, I don't. You said you're an explorer?"

"Yes, I'm really good at soaring and hunting. My vision is so keen I can see things at great distances. I know what I'm good at. That's not my dilemma. I'm not sure what I'm to do with it yet."

"Oh, I see. The journey?"

"Yes, the journey."

"You've been dreaming a lot lately?"

"Yes."

"That's how The Plan works. You dream and then you fly."

"It's that simple?"

"It is. At least, it sounds simple. It took me a while to get going until I learned something that changed my life."

"What?" the Young Eagle asked desperately.

"I had a Master Sparrow who told me that since I was born to sing that I must sing. I must not die with my songs in me. For me *not* to share my music with the world would be a tragedy."

"I know I must fly."

"Yes, you must. Just as that acorn lying on the ground must become an oak tree, you must fly. Flying will take you to your destiny."

The Young Eagle studied the smaller bird who was wise beyond her size.

"I'm not sure exactly where my journey will take me, but the eastern sky calls me."

"Then, *that* must be your destiny calling."

"I know I need to get moving. I've been hanging around here for a while dreaming."

"Dreaming is good. It's the spiritual fuel we all need to move us in the right direction. But there is something else you must know."

"What?"

"There are seasons."

"Yes, I know that."

"There is a time for hunting and a time for resting, a time for singing and a time for nest building, a time for dreaming and a time for flying."

"Are you saying that it is time for me to go?"

"Yes. You've been getting ready for a while. It's time to get busy. It's a time for doing—a time to act. Dreams without action are fantasy, simply wishes. They never become real until you act on them. Dreaming without following up is a waste of your creative intellect."

"But I was told that if I believed them, they were real for me."

"They become real when you make them real. Act on your dreams. Acting is living the dream."

"That's my fourth lesson?"

"Yes. It's time to fly."

"How did you know I would be here?"

"Destiny."

"It's all part of The Plan?"

"Yes, it is."

"What now?"

"Look to the horizon, spread your wings, and fly."

The sparrow began her song as the Young Eagle caught wind. He circled the mighty oak a few times, displaying his skill, dancing to the music of his teacher. The sparrow nodded her approval. He pitched to the eastern sky with fully stretched wings. The sparrow marveled at the broad expanse of his wings. She thought: *This eagle was born to soar to great heights and to great distances. He will fly to his destiny.*

The Young Eagle awakened to the eastern wind slapping at the branches of the tree in which the young traveler spent the night, as if the wind was announcing the birth of the morning sun. As the eastern sky called the Young Eagle to his journey, the traveler reflected on the lessons of his journey. He knew there was a plan and that he played a vital part in The Plan. He understood and accepted his unique role in this world—that he was a part of something much bigger than himself—that he was connected to everything. He felt proud and humble at the same time knowing he played a vital role in The Plan.

He embraced his special talents for soaring. He dreamed of traveling to the great unknown, to far-away places at the ends of the earth. He wanted to soar to the heavens so he could touch the face of God. He wanted to go where no other eagle had ventured before him. This was his dream. No one told him to explore; it was the voice calling to him from the deep silence in his spirit. He imagined sights that would be indescribable, and he was right. His were big and bold dreams. He knew the only reason he was able to soar to such heights was because of the grace and blessings of God. Where else could this talent, calling, and passion come from? The size of his dreams exhausted him as much as they energized him. He knew the way to realize these dreams was to act—to live what he dreamed of. *Dreams without action are fantasy*, the sparrow taught him.

As he stretched his way into this new day, he felt the stiffness in his wings. Growth often does this. The headwinds and buffeting were especially tough yesterday, and the Young Eagle did not cover as much sky as he wanted.

His thirst was as great as his stiffness. He dove to the river and drank generously. He was so engulfed in the refreshing water that he failed to notice a visitor.

"Thirsty, I see. Long journey?"

The Young Eagle turned and saw a raven perched nearby. "Yes, it has been a long trip and a tough one at that."

"How so?"

"The headwinds have been especially tough."

"So why fly into the headwinds if they're that strong?"

"Because they come from the east, and that's where I'm headed."

"What's in the east?"

"I don't know. I just know that's where I'm supposed to be. It calls to me."

The raven nodded. "I understand."

"I'm tired. This past leg of my journey has been tough."

"The headwinds?"

"Yeah, and other things. Just because a bird flies doesn't mean we don't face danger. I had an encounter with some predators while I was feeding and wondered if I would escape. They were strong, but I escaped."

"Yeah, traveling is like that. You gotta watch out for the predators. Say, you mentioned feeding. Are you hungry?"

"I could use a little something."

"Here, have some." The raven shared his morning catch with the eagle.

"Thank you. It's good."

"My pleasure. You know, most birds that stop here to refresh themselves in the water talk about the headwinds. Some quit because it's too tough; but most seem to keep going, even when they want to quit."

"I wanted to quit several times on this journey, turn around, and let the currents carry me."

"Why didn't you?"

"Because that's not where my destiny is."

"What is your destiny?"

"I don't know. Can you tell me?"

"You know that's not how it works. You have to discover that for yourself."

"What is your destiny?" the Young Eagle asked. "To feed a hungry traveler?"

They both smiled.

"In a sense."

"You're lucky."

"How so?"

"You know what you're supposed to do and where you're supposed to go. I'm not there yet. I'm still traveling."

"A lot of travelers say that. Look at the river."

"Why? What do you mean?"

"Just watch the river flow. What do you see?"

The Young Eagle stared at the water for a few moments. "I see water moving."

"Look harder. Study it."

The Young Eagle stared some more. "What am I supposed to see?"

"I've been around this river most of my life. I've learned from it. Watch how the water flows, continuously. It never stops. It moves in its own rhythm. It flows naturally over and around things. The river never thinks in terms of obstacles. It regroups and builds momentum and flows over or around the obstacles. The strength of the river flowing to its destiny overwhelms the obstacles it faces. It never completely stops. It may rest and redirect itself, but the force on the other side of the obstacles shows how powerful and determined the water is."

The Young Eagle sat there intently drinking in everything the raven said. It made sense. The persistence of the river. It continued in the face of resistance, just like the Young Eagle facing headwinds.

"Have you ever seen what happens to the water when it stops flowing? It stagnates. And occasionally, its sister, the wind, will nudge it to remind the river of its destiny. You're very much like this river, my friend. You must fly in spite of the headwinds you face. You must face these headwinds with the same courage and determination as the water faces its obstacles. As it was meant to flow, you were meant to fly. Obstacles build up force in the water and help the river find its strength. The headwinds you face help you to build wing strength for your journey. How do you feel after a tough day of winging it?"

"Tired, of course. And sore the next morning, like today."

"But it is a *good* tired, isn't it?"

"Yes," the Young Eagle conceded.

"That's growth. It's your wings strengthening themselves for the rest of your journey. The wind, even in your face, is your friend. It is helping you prepare. If it does not harm you, it makes you stronger."

"I've not thought about it that way. The headwinds do make me stronger."

"And they help you find your commitment. Every day that you do not quit brings you one day closer to your destiny. It reinforces your determination. You are stronger because of it."

"But, I've got to tell you. I was really scared of those predators."

"That's good. Fear can make you alert and vigilant. I get scared at times when I'm feeding and predators come around. That's part of courage—being afraid. It wouldn't be courage without fear."

The Young Eagle hung on to those words, "It wouldn't be courage without fear." If that's the case, then the Young Eagle had demonstrated a lot of courage in the face of the fear he had felt.

"This is lesson five, isn't it?"

"Yes. I've been waiting for you for some time. I knew the headwinds must have slowed you down a little. You're not the first to feel them."

"So, I guess my challenge is to face my challenges and keep flying?"

"Yes, especially because of the resistance. That is your challenge. Face the headwinds, be vigilant for danger, and face both with courage. You must persevere until you find your destiny. Your persistence must be greater than the resistance. By flying to your destiny, you are already living your dreams of exploring, aren't you?"

"Yes, I am."

"That's the problem too many birds have. They fail to understand that pursuing a dream is living a dream. You dreamed of exploring. You're exploring. You're living your dream right now. And all of this is happening on the way to your meeting with your destiny. Destiny, dreams, passion, and calling. When they collide, it's a spectacular and magical moment for the traveler who has become a journeyman."

"Are you sure you don't know my destiny?"

"No, that's for you and your Creator. But it is part of The Plan. You know that."

"So, what do I do now?"

"Look to the horizon, spread your wings, and fly."

The Young Eagle thanked the raven for his help and hospitality, took one more sip of water, faced east and caught air.

The next leg of the Young Eagle's journey proved most difficult. It was the great tug-of-war between the Young Eagle's past and his future—the pull of his past against the draw of his future. The farthest point from one's past is the closest point to one's destiny. He knew he must be getting close to the end, for the resistance was so great. It was his last great test to know if he was worthy of his destiny. The Young Eagle flew for weeks that turned into months and the Young Eagle accumulated experience after experience, from mountain tops to valley floors, from rain storms to desert drought. The Young Eagle met many traveling partners along the way. The obstacles, dangers, and beautiful sights forged an unyielding persistence, courage, and appreciation. On many days the Young Eagle wanted to quit, not knowing if ahead he would discover his destiny and his mission. The words of the raven rang loud in his mind: *It wouldn't be courage without fear. If it does not harm you, it makes you stronger.*

Danger lurked at every stop, but the Young Eagle would not quit. He remained true to his journey. On the days he wanted to give up, his patience, persistence, and commitment kept him flying. He remembered the words of the raven: *The river flows, continuously up and over and around obstacles, systematically wearing down things in its path.* He thought: *I must persist in the face of resistance. To quit this close to the end of one's journey must be one of life's great disappointments and failures.*

The Young Eagle struggled for hours in the face of the stiffest headwinds yet. He knew that he must be getting close to his destiny because of the unyielding force of the resistance. This energized him, but he knew he must rest if he was to continue this journey. He spied an olive tree on the horizon, it would be a good place to rest.

As he rested, the Young Eagle pierced the western sky through his sand-scorched eyes and realized how long he had been flying. He had traveled great distances for this moment. He left his family and friends to make this journey. He missed them deeply and vowed to return some day. At times, the weight of his destiny seemed too heavy a load to carry. Yet, he reassured himself that if the load felt too heavy and if it was part of The Plan, he could handle whatever appeared on the horizon. His passion for exploring and the relentless call of his destiny gave him just enough strength to persist another day. And in most cases, that's all he needed. Sooner or later, the resistance must surrender, knowing that it could not defeat the Young Eagle, that the power of his destiny was stronger than the forces that attempted to keep him from it.

"You look deep in thought."

The Young Eagle turned to face his new companion, a dove. "Yes, I've been traveling a long way. I'm tired and I miss my family and friends terribly. But I have some distance to travel before I'm finished."

"I understand. I've been waiting for you."

"Have you?"

"Yes."

"Then, I have been waiting for you, too. This must be lesson six?"

"No, actually it's not. That is still on the horizon for you."

At that, the Young Eagle slumped over on the branch, accepting the news as a heavy load placed upon his shoulders.

"Don't worry, my friend, the load is lighter than you think."

With that, the Young Eagle stretched up straight, realizing that the dove really understood what he was feeling. "How much farther must I travel?" The Young Eagle seemed resigned to the fact that he wasn't finished yet.

"You're almost there. My job is to guide you to the truth. You must trust me. Fly with me for a while."

"Where are we headed?" the Young Eagle asked, knowing the answer in his heart.

"East, to your destiny."

"What's there?"

"You will see. Patience, my friend."

"I've waited so long and traveled so far that I'm weary."

"I know. That is the way it is supposed to be. Trust me. Follow me."

With that, the dove caught air and flew east with the eagle in tow. They winged in silence for a while before the dove spoke again.

"We are almost there, hang on. Do you see that hill on the horizon?"

"Yes," the Young Eagle responded with great anticipation.

"There, my friend, awaits your destiny."

"Really?" the Young Eagle felt a burst of energy, sensing the end of his journey.

"Yes. Fly to that clump of trees. Your destiny awaits you."

"Thank you."

The Young Eagle winged as hard as he could toward the hilltop. As he got closer, he saw the clump of trees. He landed on the branch of a date palm tree and looked around. He saw little proof that he had reached his destiny. There were no other birds, no other creatures, just trees. He began to feel he had been duped, a cruel joke by nature at the end of his journey.

"You look tired, my friend."

The Young Eagle startled at the sound of a strange voice. He had heard this type of sound before, but it always signaled danger. He turned to the voice. There, beneath the tall palm, was a young man, collecting wood.

"Yes, I am tired," the Young Eagle said cautiously. "I've been on a long journey and I'm weary."

"And a little disappointed, maybe?"

"Maybe. How would you know?"

"I know."

How strange it seemed to the Young Eagle that he could understand this human and that this human could understand him.

"It is strange, isn't it?"

The young man's insight and understanding startled the Young Eagle, but the kindness of his smile and the peacefulness in his eyes comforted the Young Eagle.

"Yes. Don't you think it's odd that we understand each other?"

"Not at all. It's all part of The Plan."

The Young Eagle, reassured by these words, knew he was in the right place.

"So, you're the one?"

The young man smiled and said, "Yes, I'm the one."

"You know my destiny, don't you? You're my sixth teacher?"

"Yes, you're exactly where you're supposed to be. It's been a long journey, hasn't it?"

"I'll say! I have traveled for months for this day. My journey has been filled with excitement, disappointment, danger, and richness. I've seen things few birds could imagine. I'm tired. Reaching this point means I can let go and feel how really tired I am."

"This is a good place to rest."

"So, tell me. What is my destiny?"

"Soon. Let's talk."

"Okay. What do you want to talk about?"

"What have you been doing these past few months?"

"Traveling, exploring of course, you know."

"How does all that adventure and exploring feel?"

"It feels good. It is what I was born to do."

"Yes, you were born to soar. It is your passion and your calling. That is written in time. But there is an emptiness in you, a longing, isn't there?"

"Yes, you are wise. You know these things. I have accumulated all of these experiences and adventures but have no one to share them with."

"You have given your life to adventure, but that has been just for you. Consider this tree."

"Yes."

"It doesn't just draw sunlight and moisture from the ground. It bears fruit and offers shade. It gives back. It shares. It serves. And when it dies, it offers shelter and warmth."

The Young Eagle twitched and shivered at this. It reminded him of the nest he built and left so that other birds could use it on their journeys.

"Is that why you're collecting wood?"

"Sort of. This, my friend, is *your* destiny: Like this tree, you must serve. That is your destiny."

"That's it? I am a servant?"

"That's everything, my friend! We are all servants. The Plan calls us to serve. That's why we are all here—to serve. That is the simple truth."

"Whom do I serve?"

"Other creatures in this world. We serve one another. And by that service we ultimately serve our Creator—God."

They sat in silence for a while. The Young Eagle had to fully absorb the words of this young teacher. The Young Eagle drew in the evening air and felt energized for travel.

The Young Eagle said to the young man, "Are you here to serve?"

"Yes. I, too, serve."

"What do you do?"

"I'm a carpenter. I'm from down the road—a small town called Nazareth. That's why I need the wood. What is your name?"

"I don't really have a name."

"Yes, you do. I will call you Blessed."

"Why Blessed?"

"Because you are blessed by Our Father. He calls you to serve."

The Young Eagle sat silently on his perch. He now felt the full weight of his destiny and the load was indeed light. He now understood the greatest of truths—that we serve one another.

"That is my sixth lesson?"

"That is your sixth and most important lesson. Go now, my friend. You know what you must do, as I know what I must do."

"Thank you. I know where I must go. I must look to the western sky, spread my wings, and fly."

"Yes. Go with love and peace in your heart, for now you know your destiny."

With that, the Young Eagle caught air and headed west, to his destiny.

The Young Eagle flew for weeks to the western sky. The headwinds that slowed his journey east now propelled him west. He covered vast territory in a short period of time. The whole time he flew he replayed the lessons he had learned:

There is a plan and I'm an important part of it— a part of something much bigger than myself;

I am different and special, just like everyone else. Because of this, I possess unique talents;

To fly to my destiny, I must dream big—big enough to make my bones itch;

There is a time to dream and a time to act—I must fly;

I must persist—especially in the face and force of headwinds; and my destiny is to serve.

As he reflected on these lessons, his journey began to make sense. *The things I experienced—good and bad—were things I had to learn for me to serve in the way I will serve.* This Young Eagle felt special from the start because he felt like he fit into the scheme of things. He felt like his life had a purpose, which he discovered was his destiny. He knew he possessed unique talents for soaring and that he would use these talents to chase his big dreams of travel, adventure and excitement. And that his dreams would eventually lead him to his destiny. When he met the carpenter from Nazareth, the Young Eagle learned that serving others was his destiny. He sensed that the man he met somehow might change the world for all of time with His destiny.

Familiar sights appeared on the horizon. This energized the Young Eagle to fly even faster and stronger. There were no headwinds today, just the calm, inviting air. He reached deeper and deeper into the air pulling himself faster, as his destiny pushed him closer to the end of his journey. As he landed on a limb of the tree that housed the nest he grew up in, the youngest of dwellers in the nest kicked her feathers in excitement. The Young Eagle smiled at the play of the eaglets. He remembered how it was. As the Young Eagle stretched his wings before tucking them, he looked around for the Master Eagle. He was excited to share with him what he discovered on his long journey. He didn't see the Master Eagle.

The Young Eagle looked at the fledglings and said, "Hey, where's the Master Eagle?"

The younger birds looked at each other through sad eyes and looked down. The youngest of the nest dwellers said, "He flew west a few days ago. He said it was his time."

They all knew what this meant. This is what eagles do at the end of their journeys. The Young Eagle immediately missed his mentor, but his journey had taught him that this is the way it is supposed to be—part of The Plan.

"Yes, I understand," the Young Eagle said.

"He told us not to worry, that another Master Eagle would arrive soon to teach us what we need to know. He said that a great explorer was on his way home. He told us that this Master Eagle was one of the most skilled soaring eagles he had ever known."

At this, the Young Eagle felt truly blessed. This was his destiny, the moment for which he had prepared and waited his whole life. This was the moment when everything fell into place.

"Are you such an eagle, Mister?"

"Yes, I am such an eagle. I have returned to the nest to share with you what I have seen and done and to help you prepare for your journeys."

"Do you possess the gift of flight that the Master Eagle told us about?"

"Yes, I am blessed with that gift."

The young nest dwellers began to squirm and flap their wings with excitement, for their new teacher was here. They spit questions as quickly as they entered their minds.

"What are we supposed to know?"

"Where have you been?"

"What have you seen?"

THE YOUNG EAGLE

"Is it okay to fly in rain?"

"What's the best way to hunt?"

"Are the thermals really scary?"

"How long before we get to solo?"

"How will we know where to go?"

"How far can I travel?"

"How big should I dream?"

The Young Eagle smiled at the same innocence that once shaped his questions. Then, he recalled the words of his Master Eagle—words that he, too, would share with his students: "Look to the horizon, spread your wings, and fly."

If you would like to order additional copies of The Young Eagle book for family or friends, please call Motivation Press (636-530-0030) or log on to our website: www.TheYoungEagle.com